1 PETER

REFORMED EXPOSITORY BIBLE STUDIES

A Companion Series to the Reformed Expository Commentaries

Series Editors

Daniel M. Doriani
Iain M. Duguid
Richard D. Phillips
Philip Graham Ryken

1 PETER

GRACE-DRIVEN DISCIPLESHIP IN A DIFFICULT AGE

A 13-LESSON STUDY

REFORMED EXPOSITORY
BIBLE STUDY

JON NIELSON
and **DANIEL M. DORIANI**

P U B L I S H I N G
P.O. BOX 817 • PHILLIPSBURG • NEW JERSEY 08865-0817

ISBN: 978-1-62995-710-4 (pbk)
ISBN: 978-1-62995-711-1 (ePub)

Printed in the United States of America

CONTENTS

SERIES INTRODUCTION

Studying the Bible will change your life. This is the consistent witness of Scripture and the experience of people all over the world, in every period of church history.

King David said, "The law of the LORD is perfect, reviving the soul; the testimony of the LORD is sure, making wise the simple; the precepts of the LORD are right, rejoicing the heart; the commandment of the LORD is pure, enlightening the eyes" (Ps. 19:7–8). So anyone who wants to be wiser and happier, and who wants to feel more alive, with a clearer perception of spiritual reality, should study the Scriptures.

Whether we study the Bible alone or with other Christians, it will change us from the inside out. The Reformed Expository Bible Studies provide tools for biblical transformation. Written as a companion to the Reformed Expository Commentary, this series of short books for personal or group study is designed to help people study the Bible for themselves, understand its message, and then apply its truths to daily life.

Each Bible study is introduced by a pastor-scholar who has written a full-length expository commentary on the same book of the Bible. The individual chapters start with the summary of a Bible passage, explaining **The Big Picture** of this portion of God's Word. Then the questions in **Getting Started** introduce one or two of the passage's main themes in ways that connect to life experience. These questions may be especially helpful for group leaders in generating lively conversation.

Understanding the Bible's message starts with seeing what is actually there, which is where **Observing the Text** comes in. Then the Bible study provides a longer and more in-depth set of questions entitled **Understanding the Text**. These questions carefully guide students through the entire passage, verse by verse or section by section.

It is important not to read a Bible passage in isolation, but to see it in the wider context of Scripture. So each Bible study includes two **Bible Connections** questions that invite readers to investigate passages from other places in Scripture—passages that add important background, offer valuable contrasts or comparisons, and especially connect the main passage to the person and work of Jesus Christ.

The next section is one of the most distinctive features of the Reformed Expository Bible Studies. The authors believe that the Bible teaches important doctrines of the Christian faith, and that reading biblical literature is enhanced when we know something about its underlying theology. The questions in **Theology Connections** identify some of these doctrines by bringing the Bible passage into conversation with creeds and confessions from the Reformed tradition, as well as with learned theologians of the church.

Our aim in all of this is to help ordinary Christians apply biblical truth to daily life. **Applying the Text** uses open-ended questions to get people thinking about sins that need to be confessed, attitudes that need to change, and areas of new obedience that need to come alive by the power and influence of the Holy Spirit. Finally, each study ends with a **Prayer Prompt** that invites Bible students to respond to what they are learning with petitions for God's help and words of praise and gratitude.

You will notice boxed quotations throughout the Bible study. These quotations come from one of the volumes in the Reformed Expository Commentary. Although the Bible study can stand alone and includes everything you need for a life-changing encounter with a book of the Bible, it is also intended to serve as a companion to a full commentary on the same biblical book. Reading the full commentary is especially useful for teachers who want to help their students answer the questions in the Bible study at a deeper level, as well as for students who wish to further enrich their own biblical understanding.

The people who worked together to produce this series of Bible studies have prayed that they will engage you more intimately with Scripture, producing the kind of spiritual transformation that only the Bible can bring.

Philip Graham Ryken
Coeditor of the Reformed Expository Commentary series

INTRODUCING 1 PETER

The apostle Peter addressed his first epistle to elect men and women "in Pontus, Galatia, Cappadocia, Asia, and Bithynia" (1:1). Millions of Gentiles lived in this area—one that was larger than France or Germany—but Peter wrote to describe the privileges and life of God's *elect*. Adopting a Trinitarian framework, he declares that they have been chosen "according to the foreknowledge of God the Father, in the sanctification of the Spirit, for obedience to Jesus Christ and for sprinkling with his blood" (1:2). The Father has chosen his people, the Spirit is sanctifying them, and the Son has atoned for their sins.

Peter's **audience** is "elect exiles of the Dispersion" (1:1) or "strangers in the world" (NIV). Before God the church is "a chosen race, a royal priesthood, a holy nation," but within the empire believers are "sojourners and exiles" (2:9, 11). *Sojourner* can refer to a temporary resident, whose stay is measured in weeks or months, while an *exile* is a longer-term resident. Both words signify that a person belongs elsewhere. So the church that enjoys privileges from God suffers disadvantages within society. Gentiles will defame disciples—in part because they are "surprised" when disciples stop "living in sensuality," as Gentiles commonly do (4:3–4). Peter's readers will never be completely at home in this world.

Peter chiefly wrote to converted Gentiles. They "were ransomed from the futile ways inherited from [their] forefathers" (1:18) and their neighbors now "are surprised" (4:4) that, after years of "doing what the Gentiles want to do" (4:3), they have abandoned their lives of dissipation. Those in the churches he is writing to thus stand outside the mainstream of the empire; God's salvation has estranged them from their native culture. Peter's message is germane today, since Christians continue to feel out of place—like exiles—even in their own cultures.

Indeed, Peter became an outsider, even within Israel, after becoming a disciple. He left his home to traverse Israel with Jesus. In Acts, Peter performed miracles like Jesus and in his name (see Acts 3–4). As the church grew, the authorities threatened, beat, and jailed him (see Acts 4–5; 12). Peter tells the elect they will be outsiders too.

The exiles Peter addressed included many peoples, cultures, and languages. Peter ignored such differences and accented their status as God's elect. Jesus had shed his blood for their sin, given them eternal life, made them part of a chosen race, and changed their conduct (see 1 Peter 1:1–2:12). Henceforth, they would be exemplary citizens, servants, and spouses (see 2:13–3:7).

Exiles live between two worlds. Their new world partially alienates them from their old world and old friends. The change from pagan polytheist to Christian was great, so Christian exiles never perfectly fit in pagan society. We ourselves sense that acutely at times. Still, Peter doesn't tell anyone to abandon or curse this world. God sent his Son to redeem and restore his creation, and we should remain engaged with this world as well. We are to be ready to defend or explain our hope and our faith. We are to do good, live well, and *deserve* a positive reputation even if we never gain one (see 2:12; 3:13–17). The faith and the behavior of Christians guarantee that we will be strangers within our culture.

In many lands, Christianity is now sufficiently widespread to be able to enjoy tolerance, and even respect, but disciples cannot perfectly fit within secular societies. Still, the care of elders who follow Jesus's example (see 5:1–4) provides a place where "God's people" do fit (2:10), as we await "an inheritance that is imperishable, undefiled, and unfading" (1:4).

The **author** of 1 Peter is "Peter, an apostle of Jesus Christ" (1:1). The early church testifies that he wrote his letter while living in Rome, around A.D. 65, drawing on a lifetime of wisdom and conviction. He had walked with Jesus daily for roughly three years, experiencing everything alongside him. And this had been no accident; Jesus had *chosen* Peter to witness his deeds and words so he could then declare their meaning as his ambassador.

We thus read 1 Peter through the lens of his role as disciple and apostle. Peter was not only one of "the Twelve" (Mark 10:32; 14:10) but also a member of the inner three: Peter, James, and John (see 5:37; 9:2; 14:33).

He was a spokesman for the twelve disciples; he blurted out their worst errors and articulated their best thoughts—culminating with the declaration that Jesus is "the Christ, the Son of the living God" (Matt. 16:16; see also the rest of vv. 13–18).

After his resurrection, Jesus charged the apostles to disciple the nations (see Matt. 28:18–20). And despite Peter's failures, Jesus recommissioned him to be an apostle and commanded him to feed his sheep (see John 21:15–17). In Acts, Peter proclaimed Jesus's resurrection, and thousands repented, believed, and were baptized. Once the church was born, he testified to Christ, solved problems, rebuked sin. Then, at the Spirit's direction, he inaugurated the church's mission to the Gentiles (see Acts 10).

The books of the New Testament often state their theme at both the beginning and the end. The first of 1 Peter's **themes** is *God's grace*. Peter begins his letter, "May grace and peace be multiplied to you" (1 Peter 1:2). He closes by testifying to "the true grace of God" and telling readers, "Stand firm in it" (5:12).

This is no empty theological rhetoric! Peter's history illumines both the man and his message. He denied Jesus three times and swore that he didn't even know him. He repented in tears, and Jesus forgave him and restored him as an apostle (see Luke 22:62; John 21:15–17). Peter lived and served by grace, and he wanted the same for his people.

Peter's need of grace was most acute when he denied Jesus before the crucifixion. It is moving, therefore, that he wrote his letter with the **purpose** of helping God's elect as they are "grieved by various *trials*" (1 Peter 1:6)—a second theme. Yet trials bring more than misery and temptation. When we endure trials and remain loyal, Peter says, it proves our faith to be genuine (see 1:6–7). That brings glory when Christ is revealed. Being willing to suffer for Jesus shows we truly belong to him (see 4:1) and are standing fast with him (see 5:12). We stand fast when we remain holy in a corrupt age (see 1:14–16; 4:1–4) and when we remain loyal to Jesus through persecution (see 4:12–16).

Again, as Peter begins his letter, he tells his people that they have been chosen by the Father, sanctified by the Spirit, and sprinkled by the blood of Jesus Christ (see 1 Peter 1:1–2). God gives us grace, and we owe him obedience (see 1:2). We praise God for his mercy, for our new birth, and for the hope of an eternal inheritance with Christ (see 1:3–4, 7).

In the community of God's people, everyone receives a gift, which is also a grace (see 4:10). In love, everyone speaks and serves in ways that edify the church and glorify God (see 4:7–12). Peter has stewarded "God's varied grace" throughout his letter (4:10)—a grace that begins with Jesus's atonement (see 1:2, 18–21) and continues with assurance that he is our shepherd and overseer, even in suffering (see 2:25). Further, while Satan prowls and while brothers throughout the world suffer, "the God of all grace" pledges to restore, strengthen, and establish his people (5:10; see also the rest of vv. 8–11). The grace that Peter refers to when he closes his letter in 5:12 thus begins with Jesus's substitutionary atonement for sins (1:18–21; 2:24; 3:18–22), includes God's promise of protection in present suffering, and foretells glory with Christ in the future (see 1:6–9).

First Peter's second theme—trials and the church's faithfulness in suffering—is also prominent. Neither the empire nor the Jewish establishment persecuted the church systematically in Peter's day, but persecution was always a possibility. Christians followed Jesus, a condemned and crucified Jew who claimed to be Lord of Israel, and that could sound threatening to Rome. So every chapter of 1 Peter mentions trials and suffering (see 1:6–9; 2:18–25; 3:13–18; 4:12–19; 5:9) and the warnings grow sharper. Compare 1 Peter 3 and 4:

> Who is going to harm you if you are eager to do good? But even if you should suffer for what is right, you are blessed. . . . Always be prepared to give an answer to everyone who asks you to give the reason for the hope that you have. (3:13–15 NIV)

> Do not be surprised at the fiery trial . . . as though something strange were happening to you. But rejoice insofar as you share Christ's sufferings. (4:12–13)

In 1 Peter 3, persecution seems possible; in 1 Peter 4, it seems almost certain. Peter anticipates trouble, so he warns his churches to be ready *if* there is persecution. Later he urges his churches to see trouble in the context of their union with Christ *when* it happens.

Peter also teaches believers how to be faithful and to minimize danger in a hostile context. He calls for holiness in general (see 1:16; 2:9). Then, citing Psalm 34, he commends the behavior that makes life easier in every society—controlling the tongue, shunning evil, doing good, and seeking peace (see 3:8–12). Throughout, the church remains ready to endure. We follow Jesus's example by entrusting ourselves to God instead of retaliating when we are mistreated (see 2:21–23; 3:13–18; 4:12–16).

Although suffering is prominent throughout the letter, Peter's **focus** is first on Jesus. He "suffered once for sins, the righteous for the unrighteous, that he might bring [us] to God" (3:18)—and he did this for "the salvation of your souls," shedding his blood as a "lamb without blemish" (1:19). By this sacrifice, true members of Peter's churches "were ransomed from the futile ways inherited from [their] forefathers" (1:18).

Peter's people are now God's people (see 2:4–10), so they have broken with the pagan life they inherited from their fathers (see 1:14, 18). Yes, this makes them seem strange to their former friends (see 2:12; 4:1–4), but they are now united to Christ and heirs of eternal life with him (see 1:3–9; 4:13; 5:1–10). In every age and culture, the faithful stand against common practices when they stand with Jesus.

We see the theme of holiness amid trial throughout the **structure** of the book. After his greeting in the opening two verses, Peter praises God for granting believers new birth into a living hope (see 1:3–12). God calls his people to a holiness that rests on the redemptive work of Christ. Because God is holy, we are holy. Because Jesus ransomed us and we have tasted his goodness, we put away sin (see 1:13–2:3). Because we are God's chosen, holy nation, we abstain from sin and live honorably, even if slandered (see 2:4–12).

Holiness manifests itself socially in submission to governors and masters (see 2:13–25). Wives are to submit to their husbands, even if they are unbelievers, and husbands are to honor their wives, that they may enjoy "the grace of life" together (3:7; see also vv. 1–6). Believers can *ordinarily* expect a good life if they are good and peaceful (see 3:8–13)—though they may suffer for doing good, as Jesus did (see 3:14–22).

Jesus's example prepares believers for opposition from Gentiles (see 4:1–6). Regardless of how they are treated, disciples show self-control, love, and hospitality while using God's gifts to administer his grace (see 4:7–12). This will be necessary if we hope to face impending trials (see 4:13–19). While individual believers seek to endure and to do good, the elders of the church lead by setting an example and by overseeing everyone (see 5:1–5). In all this, believers humble themselves before God, cast their cares on him, resist Satan, and stand firm in God's grace (see 5:6–14).

Daniel M. Doriani
Coeditor of the Reformed Expository Commentary series
Coeditor of the Reformed Expository Bible Study series
Author of *1 Peter* (REC)

LESSON 1

STRANGERS WITH HOPE

1 Peter 1:1–12

THE BIG PICTURE

The opening words of Peter's first epistle make his audience clear: he is writing to "elect exiles," or strangers, of the "Dispersion." These were Christians who lived under Roman rule and belonged to various churches scattered throughout different cities and regions in ancient Asia Minor (1:1). Peter reminds them of their glorious identity in Jesus Christ: they have been foreknown by God, sanctified by the Spirit, and sprinkled with the blood of Jesus so that they might live in obedience to him (1:2). Though Peter's audience may feel like exiles in the world in which they live, they belong to the great Savior and King, who has chosen them for eternal salvation.

Peter's audience likely faced various forms of trial, trouble, and persecution as they followed Jesus in the ancient world (1:6). Though their circumstances and experiences differed, most Christians in these ancient cities faced at least some degree of social marginalization, insult, and mockery for worshiping Jesus and living holy and obedient lives for his sake. Thus Peter reminds them of the hope they have through their Savior (1:3–9). Not only has Jesus saved them, but he has also secured for them an eternal future and inheritance that cannot be shaken by any amount of earthly suffering, pain, or hardship.

Peter goes on to tell his audience that the prophets of the Old Testament "inquired carefully" into how God intended to graciously save his people; even the angels "long[ed] to look" into God's plan (1:10–12). Now the splendor of this glorious salvation has been fully revealed—both to these first-century believers and to every follower of Christ who comes after them.

Read 1 Peter 1:1–12.

GETTING STARTED

1. Have you, as a follower of Christ, ever felt out of place in your culture or community? Why might this feeling be a good sign for your spiritual health?

2. Have you ever been mocked or insulted for your belief in Jesus or in the truths of Scripture? What effect did this treatment have on your faith?

OBSERVING THE TEXT

3. How does Peter identify himself as he opens his letter? Who does he say his audience is—and what does he tell them about the identity they share (1:1–2)?

4. What is the living hope that Peter offers to these believers in 1:3–9? To what future realities does he direct their eyes and hearts?

5. Peter looks back in 1:10–12 to the witness of the prophets concerning God's coming salvation through Jesus. What does he say was significant about their witness?

UNDERSTANDING THE TEXT

6. Peter refers to his audience as earthly "exiles" in 1:1. Why are they exiles, according to 1:2? What do we learn about God's role in salvation through Peter's use of the adjective "elect" to describe the Christian exiles to whom he writes?

God's Ambassador, pgs. 4–5

Peter wrote from a lifetime of wisdom and conviction. He experienced everything, not least the trials and suffering that he describes in his letter. He also walked with Jesus every day for roughly three years. Yet Peter drew on more than experience when he wrote his epistles. He was an apostle, God's ambassador, chosen by Jesus to see his deeds, hear his words, and declare what it all means.

7. What specific actions by the three persons of the Godhead does Peter call attention to in verse 2? What do we learn from this about the work that the triune God performs for the sake of our salvation?

8. What is the "living hope" that Peter mentions in 1:3? What words does he use to describe his readers' inheritance (1:4; see v. 5 for more context)? What might have made these particular words encouraging to exiled believers in difficult situations?

9. What does Peter acknowledge is taking place in the lives of these Christians (1:6)? What does he say is the purpose of their trials (1:7)? How can this help us as well?

10. How does Peter describe faith in 1:8–9? In what sense is our salvation both a present and a future reality?

11. What does Peter say was the role of the Old Testament prophets (1:10–11)? In 1:11–12, Peter is showing that his readers have it better than the prophets of old—and even the angels. Why do they?

BIBLE CONNECTIONS

12. Read James 1:2–4, and compare it to 1 Peter 1:6–7. What additional reasons does James give for the trials in our lives? How should Christians view such trials?

13. Read Hebrews 1:1–2. How do Peter's words in 1:10–12 connect with these verses from Hebrews?

Essential Hope, pg. 15
Peter's churches, scattered through the region now called Asia Minor, suffered all kinds of trials (1 Peter 1:6). These fiery trials tested and refined their faith, but also provoked fear (3:14; 4:12). Peter assures his people that God's power will shield them. They will pass these tests, prove their faith genuine, and gain honor when their salvation is complete (1:7–9).

THEOLOGY CONNECTIONS

14. As followers of Jesus Christ, we are called to be good and faithful citizens of our earthly countries. And Peter's opening comments remind us that we are also, ultimately, citizens of heaven. How do we balance these two citizenships? How might remembering your heavenly citizenship help you to be a better earthly citizen too?

15. Answer 38 of the Westminster Shorter Catechism reminds Christians of the benefits we will receive on the day of resurrection: "At the resurrection, believers being raised up in glory, shall be openly acknowledged and acquitted in the day of judgment, and made perfectly blessed in the full enjoying of God to all eternity." What is the significance of earthly suffering or persecution in light of this future? Why should we think of this coming day more often?

Patterns, pg. 27
The prophets foretold . . . salvation, Jesus accomplished it, and the Spirit led Peter and the apostles to describe it. The pattern is *prediction* of salvation, the *fulfillment* of salvation, and the *interpretation* of saving events. . . . Scripture contains a great many things, but in essence it describes our creation in God's image, our rebellion and its catastrophic consequences, and then God's plan for restoration, announced by the prophets, and accomplished in the life, death, and resurrection of Jesus.

APPLYING THE TEXT

16. Christians today are experiencing exile just as those in Peter's audience were. What would it look like for you to live with an "exilic identity" as you worship Jesus and obey God's Word?

17. What "trials" are you currently facing (1:6)? What is tempting you to lose hope?

18. Peter tells us that our salvation has past, present, and future aspects. What encouragement can you take from this to live with hope in the midst of trials, pain, suffering, and hardship? Write down some encouraging eternal realities for you to keep in mind this week.

PRAYER PROMPT

As you wrap up your first study on 1 Peter, meditate on Peter's initial description of his audience: "elect exiles." Remember that if you belong to Jesus Christ by faith, you too are an exile—a stranger in this world. Pray that God would remind you that you are destined for an eternal inheritance in Christ that nothing in this world can shake. Praise God for the glorious and gracious gift of salvation he has offered through his Son!

LESSON 2

HOPE AND HOLINESS

1 Peter 1:13-21

THE BIG PICTURE

Peter's epistle opened with wonderful encouragement for believers who live as "elect exiles" in this world (1:1). Through Christ, they possess an eternal inheritance, a truth that should fill them with joyful hope even when they face fiery trials (1:6). Now Peter reminds his audience of the practical, daily result of this hope: lives that are characterized by holiness and obedience to God. Our heavenly mindedness should lead to holiness on earth.

Peter says that followers of Jesus who are hoping for his return must prepare their minds for action—and refuse to be conformed to the sinful passions in which they lived before their conversion (1:13-14). God's call to his faithful children is a call to holiness—just as he called the Israelites to holiness when he gave them the law of Moses to set them apart from the surrounding nations so they could offer pure worship and obedience to God (1:15-16). The motivation for this kind of holy living comes from understanding what God has done for his people in Christ: he has ransomed and saved them through the precious blood of his own Son (1:17-19). Christians live through, and for, Jesus; thus he must receive the glory as the source of the faith and hope we place in God (1:20-21).

Read 1 Peter 1:13-21.

GETTING STARTED

1. Think of a time when your expectations for a future event shaped your actions in the present. What did you do, and why?

2. In what ways are Christians tempted to conform to their surrounding culture? What temptations to conform do you face in your own life?

OBSERVING THE TEXT

3. What past realities does Peter describe in this passage?

Transformation, pg. 37

Between verses 13 and 21, Peter describes what happens when we hope in the grace of Jesus. We no longer conform to evil desires (1 Peter 1:14). We exercise self-control rather than indulging every urge. Further, because "he who called you is holy," we are holy (1:15). That leads to God's central command: "Be holy, because I am holy" (1:16, quoting Lev. 11: 44–45; 19:2).

4. Why, according to Peter, must Christians be committed to obedience and holiness? Summarize a few of his reasons.

5. What does Peter say in 1:19–21 about the value of our salvation?

UNDERSTANDING THE TEXT

6. What direct implications does 1:13 mention that our hope for the future has for the way we live in the present?

7. What does Peter say characterized his readers before they believed in Christ (1:14)? On what basis does he call Christians to pursue holiness (1:15–16)? What makes this pursuit compelling?

8. Why is God's role as judge important to those who know him as Savior (1:17)? What emotion ought we to feel regarding God as we live in earthly exile?

9. What does Peter say we have been ransomed from in 1:18–19? *How* have we been ransomed? What ought this reminder motivate Christians to do, and why?

10. In 1:20, Peter echoes themes that he covered in verses 11–12. Why does he remind his audience of these things again? What is their significance in redemptive history?

11. What are our faith and hope *in*, and where do they come from (1:21)?

BIBLE CONNECTIONS

12. Read Leviticus 11:44–45 and 19:2. What do you know about the original context and audience for these Old Testament commands? Though Peter tells us that Christ's coming has not changed this call for God's people to be holy and set apart, how does our pursuit of this holiness look different today than it did for the original readers of Leviticus?

13. Read Romans 12:1–2. What similarities and shared themes do you see between the calls and commands Paul gives to the church in Rome and the ones from Peter in our passage for this lesson? To what source of strength do both Paul and Peter refer the believer who is pursuing holiness?

Grace for the Present, pg. 39

Traditionally, we focus on the grace revealed in Jesus' life, death, and resurrection, and rightly so, since Jesus' completion of the plan of redemption brings us peace with God. Nonetheless, Peter here says that the grace to come decisively affects the present. Our hope in the grace to be revealed prepares us for self-discipline and action today.

THEOLOGY CONNECTIONS

14. In this lesson's passage, Peter calls believers to growth in holiness, known as *sanctification*. The Westminster Confession of Faith describes the process of sanctification with these words: "The dominion of the whole body of sin is destroyed, and the several lusts thereof are more and more weakened and mortified, and they more and more quickened and strengthened, in all saving graces, to the practice of true holiness, without which no man shall see the Lord" (13.1). What parts of this description remind you of the call and commands in our passage for this lesson?

15. This passage makes it clear that, though we are saved by grace and through faith in Jesus (and not by our works), the pursuit of holiness is not optional for a believer in Jesus. Why is that?

Reasons for Holiness, pg. 48
There are several reasons for a believer to be holy. First, the God who called us is holy. Second, God the Father is still God the Judge. Third, because we never fully belong in this world, we should live by God's standards. Finally, we should be holy because Jesus came to redeem us from an empty life inherited from our forefathers.

APPLYING THE TEXT

16. What hinders you from killing sin in your life and putting on righteousness and obedience? Among other things, consider to what extent misconceptions about holiness, or the lure to cultural conformity, play a part.

17. Describe some areas of your life—patterns of word, thought, or behavior—in which you need to set aside sin and pursue the holiness of Christ. Confess these to the Lord in prayer and ask him to convict you and help you to repent. Then consider some immediate changes you can make. Finally, list some Spirit-worked fruits of holiness that are already evident in these areas.

18. What would help you to focus more deeply—and more often—on the preciousness and eternal worth of your salvation? What keeps you from meditating on these things now? What motivations has this passage given you?

PRAYER PROMPT

As you close your study of this passage, ask God to fill you with hope in Jesus Christ and to give you a greater longing for his appearing. Pray for your heavenly Father to fill you with the right kind of fear—both a reverence for him and a healthy fear of the temptations and allure of this world. Ask the Spirit to fill you with grateful wonder as you consider his work in your life and heart, and ask him to help you to live a life of holiness that glorifies Christ as you wait for his return.

LESSON 3

GOSPEL PURIFICATION

1 Peter 1:22–2:3

THE BIG PICTURE

Having called his readers to be holy, Peter now instructs them on how to live in holy community with one another. Those who have been purified through their faith in Jesus Christ are called to practice "brotherly love" as an expression of their obedience to God's Word (1:22). Peter reminds them that they were saved when they responded in faith to the "living" and powerful Word of God, which endures forever (1:23–25).

Peter now calls these believers to put away every kind of sinful action and behavior that would harm the community of faith (2:1). This includes envy, slander, malice, and all relational sins that threaten to pollute the purity of gospel community. In addition, God's people should crave the pure "spiritual milk" of his Word; in fact, their appetite for God's Word, shown in their continued study and growth, will be a sign that their faith in Christ is genuine.

Read 1 Peter 1:22–2:3.

GETTING STARTED

1. What do you consider to be indications of genuine Christian faith? Explain your answer.

2. How do you view God's Word? Have you ever felt a craving or a hunger for it? Why, or why not? What did that craving lead you to do?

OBSERVING THE TEXT

3. What outward signs of genuine Christian faith does Peter mention in this passage? According to Peter, what difference should our relationship with Christ make in the way we treat his people?

Love from the Heart, pg. 54

The gospel . . . makes believers holy: "Now that you have purified yourselves by obeying the truth so that you have sincere love for your brothers, love one another deeply, from the heart" (1 Peter 1:22). To restate, Peter says that the gospel empowers moral change, specifically the ability to love our brothers "from the heart." Since the heart is "the most important anthropological term" in the Bible, this is no minor claim.

4. What truths does this passage teach about God's Word? What power does God's Word possess?

5. What does this passage command Peter's audience to do? What does it call them to turn away from? What relationship do you see between its positive and negative commands?

UNDERSTANDING THE TEXT

6. What does Peter say has been the result of his audience's obedience to the truth (1:22)? What main command does he give to them in light of their genuine saving faith?

7. What is the source of these believers' new spiritual birth (1:23)? What do you think Peter means when he describes God's Word as "imperishable [seed]" (1:23)?

8. In 1:24–25, Peter quotes from the prophet Isaiah. What point is he making about God's Word? Why should we be encouraged by the truth Isaiah expresses (v. 25)?

9. What do the specific sins that 2:1 says should be "put away" have in common? How might these particular sins interfere with Christian community and fellowship?

10. The simile in 2:2 describes the attitude that is right for Christians to have about the Word of God. What does its imagery reveal about the nature of our sanctification?

11. Why do you think 2:3 starts out with the word *if?* How does this verse serve as a warning to us?

BIBLE CONNECTIONS

12. Read Isaiah 40:6–8 and briefly take note of the verses that come before and after this section. Why do you think Peter broke into his commands to his readers with this poetic quotation? As you look at these verses in their original context, what additional insights do you gain about them?

13. Ephesians 4:31–32 contains some commands that are similar to Peter's in 2:1. Read those verses now. What do both these passages have in common? What does Ephesians 4:32 do to further develop the command we see in 1 Peter about graciously loving those who are in the community of Christ, and what does it say is the grounds for this love?

Durable Love, pg. 59

Ideally, sincere, brotherly, and earnest love come together, and we gladly help each other in the hour of need. We stick with each other when the need lasts for weeks or months. We never begrudge our labor. Love is sincere and earnest when we invite a stranded family to stay with us, and the welcome stays warm even if a dish breaks or a carpet is stained.

THEOLOGY CONNECTIONS

14. Faith is more than mental assent. The New City Catechism defines having "faith in Jesus Christ" as "acknowledging the truth of everything that God has revealed in his Word, trusting in him, and also receiving and resting on him alone for salvation as he is offered to us in the gospel."[1] In 1:22, what does Peter tell us about faith in action? How does this complement the teaching of the catechism?

15. Read 1 John 4:20. How does this verse add to your understanding of the importance of love as a sign of genuine faith?

---

1. *The New City Catechism: 52 Questions and Answers for Our Hearts and Minds* (Wheaton, IL: Crossway, 2017), answer 30.

> **Obeying the Truth, pg. 63**
> In Peter's language, if we *obey* the truth by believing the gospel, we will *tell* the truth, by putting off deceit and slander. We have tasted that the Lord is good and know that we belong to his family. God feeds us and grants us sincere, heartfelt love for each other so that we put away sin and grow up in our salvation.

APPLYING THE TEXT

16. Why is it important for you to not only accept the claims of the gospel but actually obey their truth?

17. How can you deepen your love for God's people? List at least three practical ways you can show love to those who are in your church.

18. How can you increase your appetite for the pure "spiritual milk" of God's Word? What keeps you from spending time in Scripture? What are you doing instead of reading God's Word? List some ways that you could pursue the help of God's people to engage with his Word on a deeper level.

PRAYER PROMPT

Have you received the gospel of Jesus Christ in repentance and faith? If so, your genuine love for your brothers and sisters in Christ will demonstrate the authenticity of your faith—as will your ongoing appetite for God's enduring and perfect Word. Ask God to deepen your love for his people and your desire for his Word. Thank him for the gracious salvation he has provided through Christ and for his Spirit who works in you, even now, in order to present you blameless in the end!

CHRISTIAN IDENTITY

1 Peter 2:4–10

THE BIG PICTURE

Peter wants his audience to see themselves as the people of God. What does it mean to be the church of Jesus Christ? How should they understand their calling, identity, and purpose as the redeemed people of God?

The metaphor for God's people that Peter employs throughout this brief passage is that of a house, made up of "living stones," whose foundation is Jesus Christ—the Savior and Lord of God's people (2:4–5). Those who are called to place their faith in Jesus Christ are saved as individuals, but they are called to belong to the community of faith as well—to be living stones in the house of God. Saved by grace, they are now to worship God through "spiritual sacrifices" (v. 5). God's house—the church—is built on the cornerstone of Jesus Christ, who was rejected by the world but is central to God's saving purposes for his people (2:6–8). Peter then highlights the fact that God's people have the same special calling and labels that God gave to his covenant people during the Old Testament: they are a "chosen race" (meaning "people")—a "royal priesthood" set apart to proclaim the "excellencies" of their God and Savior (2:9). All these things are true of them because of God's mercy in saving them out of darkness and calling them to be his people (2:10).

Read 1 Peter 2:4–10.

GETTING STARTED

1. What assumptions lie behind this statement: "I love Jesus, but I don't need the local church"? What could cause some people to feel this way? Yet what makes this statement incorrect?

2. How do you feel about your local church? What metaphors or pictures —whether positive or negative—pop into your mind when you think about God's people in your church community?

OBSERVING THE TEXT

3. What words does Peter use in this passage to describe his audience's identity? What words does he use to describe the way God has saved them?

4. What images, pictures, and metaphors does Peter use throughout this passage to describe Jesus? To describe his people? What do these images communicate?

5. What stands out to you about the way Peter describes the church in 2:9–10? What ideas from the Old Testament carry over here?

UNDERSTANDING THE TEXT

6. How does 2:4 describe Jesus? What contrast does Peter lay out in this verse?

7. What phrases does Peter use to describe God's people in 2:5? How do the images he uses relate to themes and ideas from the Old Testament? What is God's purpose in gathering these "living stones" together into a house?

All That Jesus Is, pg. 66
In 1 Peter 2:4–10, the apostle calls his churches "a chosen people, . . . the people of God," and imputes to them the status of a new Israel. Throughout, *Peter assumes that to come to Christ is to come into this community*: "As you come to him, the living Stone—rejected by men but chosen by God and precious to him—you also, like living stones, are being built into a spiritual house to be a holy priesthood . . ." (2:4–5). According to Peter, all that we are rests on all that Jesus is.

8. Why does Peter include the Old Testament quotation that is found in 2:6? Why is this cornerstone metaphor a fitting way to describe Christ? What promise does God give to all who believe in his Son?

9. How does 2:7–8 say that Christ the Cornerstone is treated by the world? What is the result of their treatment?

10. Do you find anything surprising or striking about the phrases Peter uses to depict the New Testament church in 2:9? What connection is there between the church of Jesus Christ and the people of God under the Old Testament covenant? What does this verse say is the purpose of the church?

Stumbling Stone, Rock, and Living Stone, pg. 68

Peter's status depends on what he says. When he forbids Jesus to go to the cross, he is a stumbling stone, but when Peter, eyewitness and apostle, proclaims that Jesus is Christ the Savior and Son of God, he is a rock. His confession is foundational for the church. When pastors proclaim the apostolic message, they build on Jesus, the prophets, and the apostles. If anyone hears this testimony and believes, he or she becomes a living stone, part of a living temple.

11. Most commentators believe that 1 Peter was written to Gentiles rather than Jews. How might that knowledge deepen your understanding of 2:10?

BIBLE CONNECTIONS

12. The rejected stone Peter describes appears in the Old Testament in Psalm 118:22–23 and in the gospels in Mark 12:1–11. Skim Psalm 118. What is the context of the rejected stone in Psalm 118? Now read Mark 12:1–11, in which Jesus quotes from Psalm 118. What point is he making?

13. The language that 1 Peter 2:9 uses to describe the New Testament church of God has its roots in God's words to his people as he prepares to give his law to his people through Moses in Exodus 19:5–6. Read those verses now. What does Peter powerfully convey by using the same words to describe those of us who make up the church today? What does this teach us about God's work throughout the generations?

THEOLOGY CONNECTIONS

14. The church, according to the Westminster Confession of Faith, "consists of all those throughout the world that profess the true religion, together with their children; and is the kingdom of the Lord Jesus Christ, the house and family of God, out of which there is no ordinary possibility of salvation" (25.2). What does it mean by saying there is "no ordinary possibility of salvation" outside the church? What part of our passage for this lesson supports this claim?

15. The Reformed theological tradition emphasizes that God's true people —in both the Old Testament era and the New—have always been saved by grace through faith, even before the first coming of Christ. What glimpse does 1 Peter 2:9 give us of this teaching?

We Share Christ's Honor, pg. 75

Jesus is the cornerstone, rejected by men, but honored by God. When we trust him, we share his honor and join his family. That is where we must find our identity. Let us define ourselves as God does. It is more true and secure, and it liberates us from self-inflicted shame. Let us remember, finally, that each calling and privilege comes from faith in Christ. We are God's chosen ones, living temples, royal priests because he is all these things first.

APPLYING THE TEXT

16. Today's passage calls us away from individualism and toward unity with the rest of God's people. As you consider your level of fellowship, community, and connection with fellow believers in Christ, has this passage challenged you to change how you act or think? Why, or why not?

17. What does the passage teach you about God's purpose for you—both as an individual Christian and as a member of his church? What can you do to better fulfill this purpose?

18. How has your study of this passage helped to grow your appreciation over God's gracious saving work? List several truths these verses teach us that give reasons for you to praise, worship, and thank Christ.

PRAYER PROMPT

If you belong to Jesus Christ by faith, you have the glorious identity of a "living stone" in the house of the eternal God, which is built on Jesus, the cornerstone. Today, pray for God to give you the strength, joy, and courage to proclaim his excellencies both to his people and to the unbelieving world around you. Ask him to teach you more about the identity you hold in Christ—not just as an individual believer but as a member of his chosen ones: the royal priesthood of the people of God.

LESSON 5

CHRISTIAN BEHAVIOR

1 Peter 2:11–17

THE BIG PICTURE

In our passage for this lesson, Peter goes on to tell his audience how to behave as Christians in an unbelieving society, and he opens his commands with some familiar language to remind his readers of the fundamental identity that marks them. God's people are "sojourners and exiles" on earth; this is our temporary home, and while on it, we are called to live faithfully for our God and Savior—both for his glory and for the eternal good of our neighbors (2:11).

Faithful exiles are called to say no to sin—to turn from sinful passions —and they are also called to practice honorable conduct among their unbelieving neighbors (2:11–12). The purpose of such holy and righteous living, Peter says, is so that the unbelievers may "glorify God on the day of visitation" (2:12). He likely has in mind their potential conversion, as well as the final vindication of God's people that will take place when Jesus Christ returns.

As they live in exile, God's people must also humbly submit to the governing authorities whom God has providentially placed to rule over them (2:13–15). He has given these authorities the role of restraining evil, and as Christians submit to them as good citizens, it should silence those who would seek to slander and critique them. God's people live in freedom—not freedom that grants them license to sin, but freedom that is grounded in the fear of God. This freedom should lead them to love one another and to respect and honor their unbelieving political leaders and neighbors (2:16–17).

Read 1 Peter 2:11–17.

GETTING STARTED

1. Do you feel like an exile or a sojourner in this world? In what ways? Describe how your faith in and obedience to Christ differentiate you from those in your surrounding culture.

2. Describe a time you saw a Christian damage their own reputation by their behavior or words. What is the impact on our Christian witness when people who claim to follow Jesus act shamefully or disrespectfully?

OBSERVING THE TEXT

3. Why is it imperative for us to "abstain from the passions of the flesh" (2:11)? Why does Peter stress that his readers must behave with holy conduct toward the pagan people around them? What do these commands demonstrate about his attitude toward unbelieving people?

4. What is surprising about Peter's commands to Christians concerning "human institution[s]" (2:13)? What might have caused these commands to be especially challenging to his original audience, who lived under the authority of the Roman empire?

5. What does this passage add to the idea of faithful citizenship that we explored in an earlier lesson? What characterizes our heavenly citizenship? What instructions does Peter give his audience about how to live as faithful citizens on earth?

UNDERSTANDING THE TEXT

6. Why do you think Peter finds it necessary in 2:11 to remind his readers of the status they hold as exiles?

Living a Beautiful Life, pg. 77
Because Jesus is Lord (1:3), all earthly lords take second place. Nonetheless, we must live beautiful lives "among the pagans" (1 Peter 2:11-12). To fashion a beautiful life, we must know how to live as free men operating in a hierarchical world (2:13-17). Thus, 1 Peter 2:11-17 reviews the *status* of believers (2:11-12) and then moves to their right *conduct* in this world—a way of life that is consistent with our identity and follows our convictions (2:13-17).

7. What is the first command that Peter gives these believers once he has reminded them of this identity (2:11)? What are the "passions of the flesh"—and why does Peter warn us against indulging in them?

8. What does Peter anticipate that some Gentiles (unbelievers) will do as his audience lives, works, and interacts with them (2:12)? In what way does he command Christians to behave among these unbelieving neighbors?

9. Why does 2:12 say believers should exercise holy conduct in the sight of unbelievers? How can their conduct serve to bring glory to God in the present? What will it do for him on the day of judgment, and why?

10. What does Peter say the Christian's mindset should be regarding governing authorities in 2:13–15? What does verse 14 say is one purpose for which God has ordained government? What is one reason verse 15 gives for Christians to humbly submit to their authorities?

11. Describe the freedom with which Peter says God's people are called to live (2:16). Whom are God's people to fear? Whom are we to love? To honor? What is significant about these word choices Peter has carefully made to describe how we are to treat each of these categories of people?

BIBLE CONNECTIONS

12. Read John 10:32–34. What do the Jews say is *not* the reason they are intending to stone Jesus, and what *is* the reason for the murderous hatred and rage they display against him? Though we should not intentionally offend outsiders through our conduct, some of them will still respond to our words and behavior in offense and anger—why is that?

13. In Romans 13:1–7, the apostle Paul issues some lengthy instructions to Christians who are living under Roman rule. Read those verses now. What similarities do you see between the instructions Paul gives to these Christians in Rome and Peter's commands from verses 13–15 of this lesson's passage? In what truths do both apostles ground their commands for God's people?

THEOLOGY CONNECTIONS

14. While summarizing his qualifications for elders in 1 Timothy 3, Paul mentions that candidates for this role of church leadership should be "well thought of by outsiders" (v. 7). Why is the reputation that a potential elder holds *outside* the church included as part of his process for qualifying for a role *inside* the church? What context does our passage from 1 Peter provide for the inclusion of this requirement?

15. The Westminster Confession of Faith summarizes the purpose of the "civil magistrate" this way: "God, the supreme Lord and King of all the world, hath ordained civil magistrates to be under him over the people, for his own glory, and the public good: and, to this end, hath armed them with the power of the sword, for the defense and encouragement of them that are good, and for the punishment of evildoers" (23.1). What purpose does God have for instituting human governments?

A New Life Estranged from This Age, pg. 77
First Peter 2 repeats the principle that God's people do not fully belong in this world. We are "aliens and strangers" (NIV) or "sojourners and exiles" (ESV) because Jesus redeemed us from a futile life and gave us a new one. By repentance and faith, we became God's people, his prized possession. By the same act, we necessarily become—and ought to remain—partially estranged from this age.

APPLYING THE TEXT

16. Where does this passage urge you, as a follower of Jesus Christ, to locate your ultimate identity? What are some practical ways you can remind yourself of the status you hold, as a "sojourner" and "exile" here on earth, when you are at work, in school, at home, and in interactions with your neighbors?

17. List three tangible ways you can present a gospel witness to your unbelieving neighbors and friends.

18. How does your attitude—or behavior—toward governing authorities need to change in response to this passage? What can you do to begin pursuing those changes in your life today?

Recognition, pg. 84

Peter promises that our good life will be recognized, even if not in this life. The pagans may glorify God for us "on the day he visits us" . . . (1 Peter 2:12). Then the Lord will review mankind and reveal all that we have done and all that it means. The pagans *might* glorify God for the beautiful lives of Jesus' disciples before then, but at least it *will* happen on the last day.

PRAYER PROMPT

As you conclude your study of this passage, ask God to make you more holy—so that you may abstain from sin and may live a life that is pleasing to him and that serves as a beautiful witness for a watching world. Ask him for the strength and desire to obey his Word. Pray for your conduct to resemble your holy Savior's so much that it would lead others to "glorify God"—either now or when Jesus Christ returns (2:12). Ask God to grant you his grace as you continue to live as a faithful "sojourner" here while also waiting for your heavenly home.

LESSON 6

THE CROSS-SHAPED LIFE

1 Peter 2:18–25

THE BIG PICTURE

As Peter continues instructing his readers on how to live as "sojourners" in the world, he commands their submission and then ties that command to the ultimate example of submission: our Savior's on the cross. He calls those who are "servants" to submit to their "masters," even if that means enduring unjust treatment—something they will be able to do both for God's glory and by his grace (2:18–20). He then offers the example of Jesus Christ as a basis for this call, since he too endured suffering, and was even wrongfully murdered on the cross, because of unjust accusations— and all without complaining or reviling (2:21–23). Followers of Christ are called to walk in his steps: to look to his example when they face unjust persecution, suffering, or abuse.

Peter closes these verses by reminding his audience that Jesus's suffering was not purposeless—that he endured the injustice and agony he experienced on the cross, and at the hands of evil men, in order to bear our sins and to heal God's people for all eternity (v. 24). God used Christ's cross to graciously restore his wandering sheep to the great Shepherd of their souls when they repent (v. 25). In the cross of Jesus Christ, we see our Savior's humility and find the means of our eternal salvation. As we follow in his steps, our lives and attitudes will be shaped by the cross as well.

Read 1 Peter 2:18–25.

GETTING STARTED

1. Can you think of times when Christians you knew *thought* they were suffering for God, or being persecuted, when they weren't? What caused their confusion? What resulted from their confusion?

2. Do you think of Jesus more often as your Savior or as an example for you to follow? Or do you give both aspects equal attention? Explain your answer.

OBSERVING THE TEXT

3. What kind of treatment does Peter assume Christians are likely to endure—and from whom (2:18–20)? Why might this be important for him to acknowledge, given his particular audience?

The Obligations of Slaves, pg. 92

After describing the social obligations of all disciples in 1 Peter 2:11–17, Peter commands, "Slaves, submit yourselves to your masters with all respect, not only to those who are good and considerate, but also to those who are harsh" (2:18). This is necessary "because Christ suffered for you, leaving you an example, that you should follow in his steps" (2:21).

4. In 2:21–23, Peter notes the example that Jesus set of enduring suffering and injustice. What reason or reasons does he give for these sufferings Jesus endured? How does he say that Jesus responded to his suffering?

5. What do verses 24–25 say Jesus's suffering accomplished—and for whom?

UNDERSTANDING THE TEXT

6. What is Peter's command in 2:18–19? What kind of attitude does he call those who work as servants (or slaves) to adopt as they follow this command—and what behavior should result? What do you think it means for a person to be "mindful of God" (v. 19)?

We Must Submit Even Today, pg. 95

Even if there is no precise analogy between slaves and free workers today, Peter's instructions do apply to all who serve harsh or perverse leaders. Evil authorities are not slave masters, but they can give harmful orders and can punish all who violate them. We should think this way: If God can command a harder thing, that slaves respectfully submit to harsh masters, surely we can submit to harsh superiors, since their power is more modest.

7. What distinction does Peter make between different kinds of suffering (2:20)? Which kind is this passage giving instructions about?

8. How does Peter say that believers should respond to Jesus's suffering (2:21)?

9. What example did Jesus set for his followers when he experienced unjust violence and mistreatment (2:22–23)? What is unusual about his response to suffering—what things did he *not* do?

Jesus Is an Example—and More Than an Example, pgs. 102–3

The imitation of Christ is a common New Testament theme. Some Protestants are wary of this. They fear that an emphasis on imitating Jesus' life might lead to neglect of his atoning death. But Jesus repeatedly presented himself as an example, especially in his endurance of unjust suffering. . . . Yet Jesus is more than an example. . . . Jesus' suffering is unique, for his death, and his death alone, is an atoning sacrifice, a penal substitution for sin.

10. What result did Jesus's suffering produce (2:24–25)?

11. What phrases in this passage call you to see Jesus as your *model* and *example*—and all the more so when you are mistreated by those in power over you? What does it do to remind you that Jesus is your *Savior*?

BIBLE CONNECTIONS

12. Read Ephesians 6:5–9. List the commands Paul gives to servants in this passage. What similarities and differences do you see between Paul's instructions here and Peter's in our passage for this lesson?

13. In Philippians 2:1–11, Paul—as does Peter, in this lesson's passage—presents Jesus as being our Savior as well as our divine example. Read those verses now. What attitudes or behaviors of Christ should we seek to emulate?

THEOLOGY CONNECTIONS

14. According to answer 27 of the Westminster Shorter Catechism, the humiliation of Jesus Christ "consisted in his being born, and that in a low condition, made under the law, undergoing the miseries of this life, the wrath of God, and the cursed death of the cross, in being buried, and continuing under the power of death for a time." What does Christ's humiliation teach us about the way we should respond when we ourselves experience shame or unjust treatment? And yet what made his humiliation so much greater than any we will experience?

15. What makes the suffering that Jesus Christ endured on the cross unique? Why is it important to understand that his suffering was unique from any other human suffering, given his identity and purpose?

APPLYING THE TEXT

16. Though the circumstances of slavery that Peter references in this lesson's passage are not completely familiar to us today, how can the principles of his command be applied to the modern relationships of employees and employers? Of students and teachers?

17. When is it hard for you to respect or submit to those who are in authority over you? How ought your attitude or behavior to change in light of what you have studied in this lesson?

18. How do you think your relationships would change if you followed more faithfully in the steps of your Savior? List some practical ways your words, actions, and thoughts could better reflect his humble heart.

PRAYER PROMPT

Ask God to give you the same heart and attitude of your Savior, who humbly submitted to unjust suffering in order to bring you to salvation. Pray for the grace to be able to submit to leaders and authorities in your life, and to respect and honor them, even when they seem unfair or unkind. Pray to be able look to your Savior—and his cross—as you do this.

LESSON 7

BEAUTIFUL WIVES; CONSIDERATE HUSBANDS

1 Peter 3:1-7

THE BIG PICTURE

Peter now focuses his instructions for followers of Christ on the most intimate of all human relationships: that between a husband and a wife. The gospel of Jesus Christ fundamentally shapes the marriage relationship: it leads wives to pursue true Christian beauty and husbands to care for and understand their wives with gentleness and consideration.

Peter first speaks to wives who follow Christ but are married to husbands who do not (3:1–2). By submitting to and respecting their unbelieving husbands, they can serve as a godly example to them—and may even win them to Christ. He goes on to encourage these women to pursue true Christian beauty—the type that comes not from any outward "adorning" but from godly character, gentleness, and kindness of spirit (3:3–6). He offers the godly example of Sarah, who submitted to her husband Abraham as she followed God by faith.

Finally, Peter turns to Christian husbands in the church and commands them to live with their wives in an "understanding" way (3:7). His use of the term "weaker vessel" to describe wives is not meant to demean them but to highlight the God-ordained complementarity between men and women in marriage. Peter concludes this passage by noting that a husband's treatment of his wife has spiritual repercussions: a man's very prayers may be "hindered" if he fails to love his wife with tenderness and care (v. 7).

Read 1 Peter 3:1–7.

GETTING STARTED

1. Why do you think submission is a distasteful idea to many? What trends and social movements have contributed to a negative reaction to that term?

2. When some Christian husbands abuse their strength and power over their wives, what makes this behavior particularly damaging to the witness of the church?

OBSERVING THE TEXT

3. What does Peter say to believing women whose husbands are unbelievers (3:1–2)? What effect do you think this would have, even if a husband's conversion does not result?

4. What does this passage say that true *beauty* consists of? Why is this important for Christian women (not to mention Christian men) to understand—particularly in cultures that celebrate outward beauty and emphasize physical attraction?

5. What kinds of behavior and attitude does Peter call Christian husbands to adopt as they interact with their wives? Why do you think his instructions for Christian husbands would have been countercultural in his day?

UNDERSTANDING THE TEXT

6. To whom does 3:1 call Christian wives to be subject? What single word puts limitations on this command?

Covenant Faithfulness, pg. 122

God's covenant faithfulness is our measure and norm. Jesus does not love the church *because* it is pure and spotless; he purifies the church in order to *make* it spotless. Similarly, husbands should love their wives as Christ loved the church—*despite* their blemishes, not *until they get* blemishes (Eph. 5:25–27).

7. What does Peter suggest may happen if Christian wives submit to their unbelieving husbands (3:1–2)? What does he say should characterize their submission?

8. What two ways of "adorning" oneself does Peter contrast with each other in 3:3–4? What does he say true beauty is all about? What qualities should godly women pursue, and what hindrances might they face in that pursuit?

9. In 3:5–6, Peter draws on the example of Sarah as he writes to Christian wives. What point is he making (3:5–6)? What did Sarah do to exemplify the kind of submission he is describing?

10. What commands does Peter give to Christian husbands (3:7)? In describing wives as both "weaker vessel[s]" and "heirs with you," what is Peter conveying about God's design for men and women from the time of creation?

11. What warning does Peter attach to the commands and instructions he gives to these husbands (3:7)? Why do you think this outcome would result from a husband's mistreatment of his wife?

BIBLE CONNECTIONS

12. Read Ephesians 5:22–33—the Bible's longest passage on Christian marriage. Which of the apostle Paul's instructions in those verses echo Peter's commands from our passage for this lesson? What connection does Paul make between marriage and the gospel?

13. Genesis 2:18–25 describes God's creation and institution of marriage. Read through that passage, and jot down some observations as you do. According to this text, why did God create Eve? How did Adam respond when he first met her?

A Command without Restriction, pg. 112

While [Peter's] command has a purpose—the winning of unbelieving husbands—it has no restriction [in the immediate context in 1 Peter]. Peter commands all wives to "be subject to your own husbands" (ESV), not men in general. Thus, *all* wives submit, and *some* have a distinct circumstance and goal—to win an unbelieving husband.

THEOLOGY CONNECTIONS

14. According to the Westminster Confession of Faith, Christians are to marry "only in the Lord" (24.6). Why is it important for Christians to seek to marry Christians? In what situations might Christians find themselves married to unbelievers, and what hope do they have?

15. Our passage for this lesson contains clear principles for Christians who are married to unbelieving spouses. Assuming there is no adultery or physical abuse, why ought Christian spouses to remain married to unbelieving spouses? How does this serve to bring glory to God?

APPLYING THE TEXT

16. Peter's instructions to Christian wives who have unbelieving husbands are a reminder for all of us that the way we conduct ourselves can serve as a witness for the gospel (3:1–2). Think of the various relationships you have with unbelievers. How might you use the lessons of this passage to shape your own thoughts and behavior?

17. What cheap ideas about beauty does Peter confront in this passage? Do you focus too much on outward beauty and physical appearance —either your own or that of others around you? What practical steps can you take to adorn yourself in the way Peter describes?

18. Peter acknowledges that the two sexes are different while also maintaining the equal value of both men and women. Why is it important for Christians today to uphold this multifaceted view of men and women?

Husbands Must Honor Their Wives, pg. 118

A Christian husband must honor women, and especially his wife. Physically, she is probably weaker, but spiritually she is a joint heir of grace. At a minimum, husbands must never bully, threaten, or strike their wives, nor should they demean their wives for being weak or slow-footed. Marriage is a union of two weak and sinful people, even if we are weak and sinful in different ways.

PRAYER PROMPT

If you are married, begin your time of prayer by considering the spiritual health of your relationship with your spouse as well as what God might be calling you to do to show more grace, gentleness, and kindness to them. Ask him to strengthen you to treat your wife or husband as a fellow heir—and pray that you will help, and not hinder, their walk with Jesus Christ. If you are not married, pray that the marriages of believing friends and family members would be strengthened and nourished by God's grace. Ask him to give you the desire to pursue godly, internal beauty rather than a mere outward adornment.

LESSON 8

THE GOOD LIFE AND THE RIGHT FEAR

1 Peter 3:8–18

THE BIG PICTURE

Peter's instructions to his audience demonstrate that these "elect exiles" are likely to face scorn, ridicule, and mockery for their worship of the one true God. Their allegiance to Jesus as their ruler sets them apart from their unbelieving neighbors and surrounding culture. Yet Peter writes that their pursuit of goodness and kindness should generally win them favor—and if they do suffer for living faithfully, they should remain ready to entrust their lives and souls to God, who allowed his own Son to suffer in their place.

Peter calls these believers to exhibit godly qualities in their lives and relationships (3:8). When they face reviling from others, they should "bless" them in return (3:9). The normal consequence of living this kind of life will be God's blessing—a truth Peter demonstrates by quoting from Psalm 34 (3:10–12).

Yet Peter says that his audience may face suffering and mistreatment even if they are living godly lives and speaking lovingly and humbly. In such cases, they should not fear those who are persecuting them but should trust in God and remain ready to give clear answers about Jesus—even to those who seek their harm (3:13–16). Peter reminds these Christians that it is sometimes God's will for them to suffer for good. After all, his own Son suffered "once for sins" (v. 18) to bring sinners from death to life (3:17–18).

Read 1 Peter 3:8–18.

GETTING STARTED

1. Describe times you have seen people of godly character and integrity receive blessing and favor on earth. Then give some examples of Christians you know who are respected by unbelievers.

2. Now think of some historical examples of Christians who underwent persecution, hatred, and mistreatment, yet humbly loved those who hated them. What biblical figures also suffered in this way?

OBSERVING THE TEXT

3. What principles does Peter describe in 3:8–12. For those who follow them, what blessings can be generally expected to result? Why?

A Good Life Allows Peace, pg. 125

A good life allows peace. Whatever we may say about life in an alien culture, under hostile authorities, the greater part of the Christian life concerns the character and disciplines that shape daily actions and our universal responsibilities. So Peter describes the virtues that bless everyone: harmony, sympathy, love, compassion, and humility.

4. What does Peter acknowledge may happen even if God's people are showing love to those around them? Why was it especially important for him to acknowledge this possibility for his original audience, who were living under the rule of the Roman empire?

5. What source of hope does Peter point his audience to as they prepare their hearts and minds for suffering?

UNDERSTANDING THE TEXT

6. What do all the qualities that Peter tells his audience in 3:8 to pursue have in common? How would these qualities help them in a time of persecution?

7. What does 3:9 say that followers of Jesus should do in response to evil or reviling? What promise does it connect to this command?

8. Why do you think Peter chose to quote verses from Psalm 34 amid his instructions to Christians in the first-century Roman empire (3:10–12)? What general principles and promises does his quotation lay out?

9. Peter indicates that a commitment to righteous, good, and holy behavior will generally keep Christians away from "harm" (3:13). Yet what possibility does he go on to acknowledge in the next verse? How does he begin to prepare his audience for that possibility?

10. What "fear" should followers of Jesus reject (3:14)? What does 3:15 present as the alternative to such fear? What is one outcome of our faithful suffering and our witness for Jesus Christ (3:16)?

11. What role does God play in the suffering that Peter describes in 3:17? What does Peter tell us about faithful endurance under such suffering?

BIBLE CONNECTIONS

12. Read Psalm 34:11–22, and note the passage's broader context. What general principles found within this psalm have you seen playing out in the world around you? After what verses 11–18 say, does anything seem surprising about verse 19? What ultimate hope does this psalm say the righteous servants of God can look forward to?

13. Skim through the account in Acts 4:1–22 of when Peter and John are brought before the Jewish elders and scribes. What do they do to demonstrate "gentleness and respect" to their accusers (1 Peter 3:15) even though they are disagreeing with them and refusing their orders to stop speaking about Jesus?

We Never Quite Fit, pg. 125

If we act in [the ways described in this passage], Peter says that we can ordinarily expect to live well and enjoy God's favor. He asks, "Who is going to harm you if you are eager to do good?" (1 Peter 3:13). The next section admits that it *is* possible to suffer harm for doing good (3:14–17). If we live by God's standards, we will never quite fit into any human culture. This was true in the empire, where the Christians' allegiance to Jesus as Lord and refusal to worship the emperor could be taken as a sign of dissent.

THEOLOGY CONNECTIONS

14. The theologian Dietrich Bonhoeffer was arrested and executed for opposing Adolf Hitler. He once said, "Those who are afraid of men have no fear of God, and those who fear God have no more fear of men."[1] Review Peter's command in 3:14–15. What attitude do both Peter and Bonhoeffer say should characterize our commitment to Christ?

15. After calling his audience to prepare to suffer in exchange for doing good, Peter reminds them of the *once-for-all* suffering that Jesus Christ endured on the cross (3:18). Why is it important for us to remember Christ's suffering, as well as what it accomplished? What causes our suffering to be different from our Savior's while still connected to it?

---

1. Quoted in Daniel Doriani, *1 Peter*, Reformed Expository Commentary (Phillipsburg, NJ: P&R Publishing, 2014), 139.

We Will Suffer, pg. 143

The disciple, wrongly accused, might suffer unjustly. . . . If we suffer for doing evil, we merely endure just punishment. A believer cannot claim persecution when punished for wickedness or folly. But if we suffer for doing good, we demonstrate our union with Christ and can expect to join him in glory (4:13–14). Until then, we strive to live well and endure suffering "if it is God's will."

APPLYING THE TEXT

16. What is your response to Peter's command not to return "evil for evil" or "reviling for reviling" (3:9)? Have you ever fired back harsh words at people who insulted you or spoke ill of you? What ought you to remember when this happens so that you bring glory to your Savior?

17. What people or things inordinately trouble you? Are you ever tempted to fear them more than you fear God (3:14)? What actions can you take to cultivate a stronger fear of the Lord?

18. Why is it important to reflect often on the hope that the cross gives you, because of the suffering Jesus faced on it "once for sins," as part of your preparation for experiencing the hardship and suffering you yourself will face as a Christian (3:18)? How did Christ's suffering make him into both a model and a representative for you?

PRAYER PROMPT

Begin your prayer for this lesson by asking God to strengthen you for the task of speaking of the hope you have placed in Christ Jesus. Pray also that you would fear him above all else. Ask his Spirit to give you the grace to live in gentleness, kindness, and humility—ready to suffer with your Savior, if that is his will for you. Take time to praise him for the suffering that Christ perfectly endured on your behalf—suffering that has reconciled you to God.

LESSON 9

CHRIST'S WORK AND OURS

1 Peter 3:18–4:6

THE BIG PICTURE

Having called his readers to remain faithful during earthly suffering, Peter now describes the powerful work Jesus Christ accomplished through his death, resurrection, and ascension (3:18–22). Although this section of Scripture contains verses that are among its most difficult, the passage's main point is clear: Jesus has triumphed over his enemies and achieved victory for the sake of his redeemed, forgiven, and baptized people. Peter tells us that between his death and resurrection, Jesus made some kind of proclamation to the "spirits in prison," over whom he now rules eternally (vv. 18–20). He then contrasts these disobedient spirits with the faithful followers of Jesus who are marked by baptism—a sign of the saving work God has done in them through Christ, and one that harks back to the merciful salvation he granted to Noah and his family in the midst of his judgment (vv. 21–22).

Next, Peter describes the implications that Christ's saving work has for believers' attitudes regarding sin and temptation (4:1–6). Christ's suffering is supposed to serve as an inspiration for God's people to put their sin and "human passions" to death (vv. 1–2). Peter emphasizes that his readers have turned away from the sinful pleasures that formerly gripped their hearts and lives—a shift that has invited mockery and maligning words from their unbelieving neighbors (vv. 3–4). He also focuses the eyes of Christians on the final day, when unbelievers will be judged and those who live by the "spirit" will be vindicated by their faithful God and Savior (vv. 5–6). The challenging phrase in verse 6 about how the gospel was "preached even to those who are dead" likely refers to those who were physically dead, at the time Peter was writing this letter, but who were converted before their deaths and vindicated by God, despite being judged by the unbelieving world.

Read 1 Peter 3:18–4:6.

GETTING STARTED

1. Sometimes Christians view the work of Jesus Christ (his death and resurrection) in an overly individualistic way. Why is it important for us to consider *all* the implications of his work—those not just for us as individual Christians but for the whole universe (for the physical creation, for Satan and his servants, and so on)?

2. What bogs down your pursuit of holy living and your obedience to God's Word? Are there sins plaguing your life over which you can't seem to triumph? Why do you think this is?

The Course of Life Is Open, pg. 161

In the end we have one broad goal—to live "for the will of God" (1 Peter 4:2). There is a point of departure, the debauchery and idolatry of our pagan past (4:3). And there is a goal—the day we meet the Judge and account for ourselves (4:5). Other than that, the course of life is open as we leave sin behind and follow Christ.

OBSERVING THE TEXT

3. Peter encourages his audience by referring in this passage to one of the works that Christ accomplished—which is it? Identify specific things he says to strengthen the faith of God's people and firm up their resolve to faithfully obey his Word.

4. What does Peter say in this passage to challenge and exhort his audience? What temptations does he confront?

5. Are there details within this passage that you find difficult to interpret? Write down anything in these verses that confuses you or leaves you with questions. Does reviewing the context of the rest of the passage bring any more clarity to its difficult sections?

We Will Be Vindicated, pg. 148

Whatever the uncertainties in 1 Peter 3:18–19, the main theme is manifest: When Jesus suffered unjustly, God vindicated him, and he will vindicate us, too. . . . Jesus was put to death, and then rose to life and ascended into heaven. Peter wants us to know that if we suffer and even die for the faith, God will raise and vindicate us, too.

UNDERSTANDING THE TEXT

6. In 3:18, Peter describes the once-for-all work that Jesus Christ performed on the cross. What makes his suffering absolutely unique? What does Peter say that it accomplished for God's people?

7. What seems to be the purpose of the proclamation that 3:19–20 says Jesus made to "the spirits in prison"? What behavior does Peter assign to these spirits?

8. What does Peter say in 3:21–22 is the purpose of Christian baptism —what power does it have? What do we learn about the significance of baptism when we read these verses?

9. What does Peter say should motivate us to be holy (4:1–2)? What do you think it means to live "for the will of God" (v. 2)?

10. According to 4:3, in what manner did many members of Peter's audience likely live before they came to faith in Jesus Christ? Why do you think he is urging them to put that life behind them? What reaction does 4:4 tell them to expect from their unbelieving friends and neighbors as they do so, and why?

11. What will happen to those who "malign" and mock believers for obeying Jesus Christ (4:5)? What ultimate vindication is in store for God's people, even if the unbelievers around them judge them for now (4:6)?

BIBLE CONNECTIONS

12. Read Colossians 2:13–15, and note what effect Paul says Jesus's sacrificial work on the cross accomplished. What connection do you see between these verses and the triumphant proclamation that 1 Peter 3:18–19 describes Jesus making?

13. Read what Jesus says about his second coming in Matthew 24:43–44. How does he describe the nature of the judgment he will bring to the world? What does he call his people to do in response to his words? What possible influence on 1 Peter 4:5–6 do you see in the Matthew passage?

THEOLOGY CONNECTIONS

14. Daniel Doriani explains the "most widely adopted" interpretation of 1 Peter 3:19: that after his death, Jesus "made a proclamation to fallen angels"—perhaps an announcement that his "death, resurrection, and exaltation sealed their defeat and doom."[1] If this was indeed the substance of his triumphant proclamation, what encouragement should we take from it? What does it add to our understanding of the victory Christ won?

1. Daniel Doriani, *1 Peter*, Reformed Expository Commentary (Phillipsburg, NJ: P&R Publishing, 2014), 152–53.

Breaking the Power of Sin, pg. 168

We can trust God to write new lines and let the story unfold as he wills. That begins with the substitutionary sacrifice of Christ, and then to his exemplary life that shows the way. It continues with Jesus' resurrection and ascension. These grant us the boldness that lets us break with our old life. The world may slander, but it is more than enough compensation to share the attitude of the Lord who broke the power of sin on the cross, that we might break the power of sin day by day.

15. The Westminster Confession of Faith explains that baptism is a sacrament "ordained by Jesus Christ" to enable the entrance of the "party baptized into the visible church . . . a sign and seal of the covenant of grace, of his ingrafting into Christ" (28.1). What does this explain about Peter's assertion that baptism saves those who are baptized? What *connection* does baptism have with salvation and with a person's entrance into God's covenant community? How does it help to remind you of your new identity and strengthen you to obey Christ?

APPLYING THE TEXT

16. Does the first part of this passage (3:18–22) expand your view of Jesus Christ's triumphant work? If so, what does it add to it? In what ways can these verses help to dispel your fear of Satan and his servants?

17. What does Peter say will happen if you refuse to take part in the sinful actions or attitudes of your culture? What practical preparations can you take to be able to endure this kind of treatment?

18. Why is it important for you to remember that God seeks your *holiness* as well as your happiness? What do you need to do, right now, to put to death the sinful thoughts, words, and attitudes that remain in your life and your heart? How does the suffering of Jesus inspire you as you do this?

PRAYER PROMPT

As you conclude your study of this passage, spend some time thanking God for the work of Jesus Christ, who suffered in your place and proclaimed victory over Satan, sin, and death. Pray to effectively "arm" yourself to suffer with and for Jesus, the way he suffered in the flesh, and to seek to put to death the sin that tempts you—the sin for which your Savior died. Praise God for the victory you have through Christ—both now and forever!

LESSON 10

GIFTS FROM GOD; GIFTS FOR GOD

1 Peter 4:7–11

THE BIG PICTURE

In this lesson's passage, Peter's set of instructions focuses on how the believers are to use their *gifts*—namely, for the good of their brothers and sisters in Christ and for the glory of Jesus, their Savior and Lord.

Peter precedes these instructions with a reminder that the return of Jesus Christ will take place soon—that, as he says it, that day of judgment is "at hand" (v. 7). In light of the fact that Jesus's return is imminent, Peter calls his audience to live lives that are marked by self-control and by the love they share together within the body of Christ (4:7–9). The prospect of his return and of the day of judgment should lead Christians to live out practical holiness, gracious love for one another, and the joyful practice of hospitality (v. 9).

Peter goes on to tell his readers that God's people have received their gifts from him and are to use them fittingly as stewards of his grace (4:10). Whatever a person's gift or ability may be, Peter commands him or her to use it for the glory of Jesus Christ (4:11).

Read 1 Peter 4:7–11.

GETTING STARTED

1. What are some popular portrayals of ways for an apocalypse or the end of the world to play out? If you knew the day of final judgment would come *tomorrow*, what would you do today?

2. What misunderstandings about spiritual gifts do you think are present in the church today? What questions do *you* have about them?

OBSERVING THE TEXT

3. How does Peter open verse 7? After this dramatic beginning, does anything surprise you about the commands that follow in 4:7–9? What sort of instructions might you have expected instead?

Making Our Gifts Fruitful, pg. 170
We can feel that we are made for something when we exercise our God-given gifts. Gifts equip believers for service in God's kingdom—for the church first, but also for work in the wider world. . . . God grants *abilities* to all people, believers and doubters alike. These abilities become gifts when we dedicate them to God and the Spirit wills to make them fruitful for his purposes.

4. What does Peter say is the source of our gifts and abilities? What does he say to make this clear?

5. What guidance does this passage provide regarding the right way for Christians to order their priorities in view of Jesus Christ's coming return? How can it serve to encourage "ordinary" Christians in the church?

UNDERSTANDING THE TEXT

6. What does Peter indicate is true about the "end" to which he calls his readers' attention in 4:7? How are we—who are living two thousand years after Peter wrote these things—to understand this?

7. What does Peter call his audience to do, later in verse 7? What reason does he give for commanding these things?

8. Why is the command in 4:8 such a fundamental one for Christians to follow? In what sense does Christian love cover over sins? What does that look like when practiced in the church community? Why do you think Peter mentioned hospitality after telling his readers to love one another (4:9)?

9. What are Christians responsible for doing with the gifts God has entrusted to them (4:10)? Why?

10. Peter mentions two specific gifts in 4:11. Why might the gifts of speaking and serving be particularly important to the healthy life of a church?

11. What does 4:11 say is the ultimate goal behind Christians' use of their gifts? Does this change your perspective on how and why we use our gifts as members of our Christian community?

BIBLE CONNECTIONS

12. Read Revelation 22:11–14. What does Jesus say about when his second coming will occur? What are the implications of when we can expect his return?

13. Read 1 Corinthians 14:1–19, which lays out some principles for how the gifts of prophecy and tongues can be applied within the church. What are some of the central commands Paul lays out regarding the use of these gifts? What is the most important aspect of employing these particular gifts?

We Live in the Last Phase of Redemption, pg. 171

When this age ends, Jesus will return to overthrow sin and establish his new order. That day is near in the sense that it could happen at any time. . . . "Therefore," Peter says, we must live in light of Jesus' return and be clear-minded, self-controlled, prayerful, and full of love and forgiveness (1 Peter 4:7–8). Because we are in the last phase of God's plan of redemption, because the end is near, certain conduct follows.

THEOLOGY CONNECTIONS

14. The Westminster Confession of Faith calls believers, as Peter does, to remain ready for the imminent "end of all things"—the return of Jesus Christ—when "the bodies of the unjust shall, by the power of Christ, be raised to dishonor: the bodies of the just, by His Spirit, unto honor; and be made conformable to His own glorious body" (32.3). Why should Christians think of this day often and look forward to it hopefully and expectantly? What should the reality that this day is coming motivate us to do?

15. Much confusion about spiritual gifts abounds today. What Peter seems to think is most crucial for Christians to understand is that their gifts, whatever they are, both (1) come from God and (2) are to be used for his glory and for the good of fellow believers in the church. Why is it important for us to keep both the source and the purpose of our gifts in mind?

Gifts and Graces, pg. 177

Scripture calls our capacities *graces* because they are more than abilities. God gives them graciously, and they are *means* of grace for others. Peter says that the gifted "serve others, faithfully administering God's grace in its various forms" (1 Peter 4:10). At best, gifts empower us to do God's work and focus our attention on him and his grace. . . . We distinguish the abilities possessed by the godless from the gifts of believers this way: we seek the glory of God as well as the "common good" (1 Cor. 12:7).

APPLYING THE TEXT

16. How often do you think about the second coming of Jesus Christ? What can you do to remind yourself, and others, to think about his return more often? What sometimes makes it difficult to see the end of all things as being imminent? Why is it important for you to take this perspective regardless?

17. What practical things can you do to increase your love for fellow believers? List some ways you can show hospitality to those in your community and church.

18. What gifts and abilities has God given to you? Are you using them for his glory and for the good of fellow believers? If so, how? If not, what is holding you back?

PRAYER PROMPT

Begin your prayer by asking God to give you his perspective on the imminent return of Jesus Christ, his Son. Pray, as that day draws near, that you would increasingly practice self-control, obedience to God's Word, love for his people, and gracious hospitality. Ask him to give you the desire to love and serve his people, even when doing so is difficult. Then praise God for the gifts he has graciously entrusted to you, and ask him for the strength to steward them well—for his glory and for the good of the church!

LESSON 11

GOD'S WAY TO ENDURE TRIALS

1 Peter 4:12–19

THE BIG PICTURE

Peter began to prepare his audience, earlier in his letter, for the possibility that they may suffer for and with Jesus Christ, and now he addresses the reality of the persecution that some Christians are already facing. He longs to help these dearly beloved believers to endure suffering with faith and hope and, even in the midst of trials, to look to the day of judgment when their Savior will return.

He begins by telling his readers that they should not be "surprised" when trials and suffering come (4:12). In fact, Christians' attitudes about suffering and persecution should lead them to rejoice if they happen, because this means that they are sharing in the sufferings of their Savior and have been counted worthy of being identified with him (4:13–14). Peter clarifies that the suffering he is writing about is not the consequence of a person's own sin or unwise choices and that no Christian should bring about suffering because of his or her own wrongdoing (4:15). But, when believers suffer with Jesus as a result of their obedience and faithfulness to his gospel, they should praise God for being given such a privilege (4:16).

Peter ends this passage by reminding believers of the eternal hope they have: that God will return in glory and will reign over all (4:17–19). Since they know that judgment is coming for the entire world, Christians should prepare themselves for the day when they meet their Savior face-to-face. Their hope of being finally vindicated and resurrected to life is what

95

ultimately strengthens believers to continue to "entrust" their souls to a faithful God—even when they are enduring great hardship on earth (4:19).

Read 1 Peter 4:12–19.

GETTING STARTED

1. Are you surprised when trials and suffering arise in your life? If a believer is truly expecting not to experience these things, what wrong beliefs might such a person have about the Christian life?

2. What does the example Jesus set through his life and ministry tell us about what we should expect from the Christian life? What does the world tell us to expect, and strive for, during this life?

OBSERVING THE TEXT

3. What instruction does Peter give his readers as this passage begins (4:12)? What kinds of suffering might his original audience have been enduring?

4. What attitude does Peter invite his readers to take up when they experience suffering (4:13)? What reasons does he give for making this shift in their perspective?

5. What future event does Peter mention to his audience? How should their perspective on their present sufferings be shaped by the reality of this event?

UNDERSTANDING THE TEXT

6. What do you think would have "surprised" Peter's audience about the trials they had begun to experience (4:12)? What incorrect assumptions might they have been holding about what following Jesus on earth would be like? What does Peter say to correct their thinking?

A Shift in Tone, pg. 188

Perhaps, as some scholars speculate, Peter received bad news even as he wrote [his first epistle]. Whatever the reason, Peter's tone shifts in chapter 4. Suffering was a possibility; now he urges his readers to expect trouble. In 1 Peter 3:13–17, Peter tells us that persecution will possibly happen and that disciples must be prepared if it does. In 4:12 he says, "Do not be surprised at the painful trial you are suffering."

7. What cause does Peter offer for rejoicing amid suffering (4:13–14)? In what sense is being persecuted for the sake of Jesus's name actually a blessing and a sign that God's grace is upon a person's life? What allows such suffering to encourage a Christian's faith rather than to damage it?

8. To what kind of suffering is Peter *not* referring (4:15)? Why is it important for us to know the difference between these two types of suffering and not to confuse them—in our lives and in the lives of others?

10. What two kinds of "judgment" does 4:17–18 present? In what sense are God's people who make up the church judged *now*? What is the difference between this earthly judgment that God's people face and the final judgment that awaits the ungodly?

Danger Ahead, pg. 189
The leaders of the Roman Empire were not necessarily hostile to religious divergence, but new religions, exclusive religions, and rapidly growing religions were viewed less favorably. The apostle warns of trouble because he sees it coming and wants to shepherd his people. If they are prepared for adversity, they can endure, possibly even thrive. As we read Peter, we hear an urgent personal word. He wants to warn his "dear friends" of an imminent danger.

11. What concluding command does 4:19 offer to suffering Christians? What is Peter emphasizing about God in this verse, and why would that emphasis be helpful to his readers?

BIBLE CONNECTIONS

12. Read Acts 5:40–42. Why clues does this passage give us about why Peter and John are flogged? How are they shown to be following the commands within 1 Peter 4:12–19? What specifically about their situation do they find to be worth rejoicing over?

13. Read Colossians 1:24. What does Paul understand to be the reason or purpose for the suffering he is enduring? What does this verse add to the principles that we saw in 1 Peter 4:13–14?

What Do Our Words and Deeds Reveal? pg. 198
The believers' sins and failings will be forgiven, yet—what a gift—our noble words and deeds will attest our heart commitment to the Lord on judgment day. . . . Therefore, we should examine ourselves and ask what our words and deeds reveal. Do they show that Jesus is our King and that his grace and reign have transformed us? Peter directs us to expect that day and prepare for it, living according to our identity as members of "the family of God"—the Father's sons and daughters.

THEOLOGY CONNECTIONS

14. The "health and wealth" gospel, or "prosperity gospel," is a teaching that generally posits that faith in Jesus will lead to earthly comfort, material wealth, worldly favor, or physical health (or even all of them together). The Bible never promises us these things—we are following a Christ who himself faced suffering when he died on the cross for our sins. What can you do to confront this false "gospel" when you hear it? Do you think this kind of teaching has a grip on people you know? Why, or why not?

15. The Westminster Confession of Faith explains that "God does continue to forgive the sins of those that are justified; and although they can never fall from the state of justification, yet they may, by their sins, fall under God's fatherly displeasure... until they humble themselves, confess their sins, beg pardon, and renew their faith and repentance" (11.5). What is the difference between being persecuted and experiencing God's fatherly discipline? What additional clarification does this quotation offer regarding the important distinctions that 1 Peter 4:13–16 makes?

APPLYING THE TEXT

16. Do you have expectations regarding the Christian life that need to be changed or reexamined now that you have read this passage? What is the problem with the mindset of Christians who expect to enjoy only comfort and worldly success?

17. Why must we be careful about calling the suffering we (or others) experience for our sinful actions, or unwise choices, "persecution"? What should be our response to suffering that results from our own sin, stubbornness, or unwise choices?

18. Do Peter's commands within this passage convict you about trusting God more deeply? Does the passage challenge the current perspective you take to your experiences with earthly trials and suffering? What can you do to nurture an eternal perspective on such experiences? Do you think reflecting on the final judgment would help to fuel your obedience to Jesus? Why, or why not?

PRAYER PROMPT

Conclude your study of this passage by praying for God, in his grace, to help you to adjust your expectations regarding the Christian life. Ask him to remind you not to be surprised when you suffer or face hardship because of Jesus's name. Pray for the strength to rejoice if, and when, you are insulted or marginalized for the sake of the gospel. Finally, ask God to strengthen your faith and to found it more strongly on the knowledge that the risen and reigning Savior will vindicate you, in his presence, on the last day.

LESSON 12

SERVANT LEADERS FOR
THE SHEPHERD JESUS

1 Peter 5:1–4

THE BIG PICTURE

Peter begins chapter 5 of his epistle with an address that's specifically for the elders of the churches to which he is writing. These church elders are men who have been called to lead, teach, and shepherd these different local congregations—to care for and serve God's people faithfully and with integrity. Peter's address to these men contains commands concerning the motivation they should have for leading, the manner of service they should render to God's people, and the ultimate perspective they should take to their role: that of shepherds under the rule of the "chief Shepherd," who will one day return.

Early in this address, Peter counts himself an elder along with these men—one who has shared in and witnessed the sufferings of Christ and who is looking forward to the glory that will belong to all God's faithful people (5:1). He then offers three pairs of contrasting approaches to church leadership. First, he says godly elders are to lead willingly and not under compulsion. Next, they are to undertake their elder roles not for selfish reasons or from greed but out of an eagerness to serve God's people (5:2). Finally, they are not to domineer over God's people but rather to serve as godly examples for them (5:3). All of this is to be done with a sense of accountability to the "chief Shepherd," Jesus Christ himself. Those who have faithfully served in this role can look forward to being handed a "crown of glory" by their Shepherd when he returns (5:4).

Read 1 Peter 5:1–4.

GETTING STARTED

1. What selfish motivations tend to drive Christian leaders to fall into sin or to abuse or neglect the people they are called to serve? What specific temptations arise from leadership, power, and authority?

2. What does your culture assume makes a great leader? Which of its assumptions run contrary to the qualifications that the Bible gives for a leader in the church?

The Suffering of Godly Leaders, pg. 202

Through Scripture, godly leaders have witnessed Jesus' sufferings. Depending on their age and course of life, they see, whether dimly or fully, what it means to suffer with him. They also hope to share in his glory, and depending on their age and experience, they have either robust or guarded optimism about their chances. But whatever their expectation, they hope to shepherd God's flock by their teaching and a godly example.

OBSERVING THE TEXT

3. To whom is Peter addressing the verses in this passage? In what sense do his commands apply to him as well?

4. What sinful motivations does Peter mention can lie behind a person's leadership? How does it help us to be aware of these wrong motivations? What godly motivations does Peter provide as a contrast to these?

5. In what part of this passage does Peter call his readers' attention, once more, to the day of Christ's return? How should the fact that Jesus is coming impact the way an elder understands his duty to the people in his church?

UNDERSTANDING THE TEXT

6. In 5:1, what does Peter say qualifies him to be an apostle and an elder? What connection did he have with the sufferings of Christ? What hope for the future is he clinging to?

7. What would it look like for a leader to serve "under compulsion" (5:2)? What does it look like, by contrast, to serve and lead God's people willingly?

8. What opportunities do Christian leadership positions contain for the "shameful gain" that that same verse implies might draw people to them? What would cause a rightly motivated elder to serve God's people "eagerly" instead of from such a sinful desire for gain? How can the hope that the gospel offers be a motivation for someone to serve in such a way?

9. What does it look like when leaders domineer over those who are under their care (5:3)? Why is domineering leadership harmful to a church? What kind of leadership does Peter command elders to exercise as an alternative? What makes it a better way for them to lead?

10. Peter describes Jesus Christ as our "chief Shepherd" (5:4). What implications does this description have for all members of the church —and what implications does it hold for church leaders in particular?

11. What reward does Peter speak of in 5:4? Why is it important to note that this is a heavenly reward rather than an earthly one? What implications does that distinction have on what men should expect when they are called to lead the church?

BIBLE CONNECTIONS

12. Read 1 Timothy 5:17–18. How does this passage say members of the church should treat the elders who are called to lead God's people?

13. Read Titus 1:5–9. On what points do the commands Peter gives *to* elders in our passage for this lesson, and the qualifications Paul passes along to Titus for men who are seeking to *become* elders, overlap with each other?

No Christian Leader Is Self-Qualified, pg. 206

The lessons are clear. First, no Christian leader is self-qualified, morally or spiritually. No one deserves to lead the church. Jesus forgives, appoints, and qualifies his apostles and elders. Second, the core of an elder's qualification is the love of Jesus, both experienced and returned. The love of Jesus creates the essential desire to lead and care for God's people.

THEOLOGY CONNECTIONS

14. Denominations like the Presbyterian Church in America and the
    Orthodox Presbyterian Church have rigorous requirements for all
    those who are seeking to be licensed and ordained as pastors. And
    churches in these denominations examine, train, and test men who
    have been nominated for the office of elder or deacon as well. What
    influence should churches take from this lesson's passage regarding the
    way they examine potential officers' *motivations* for ministry leadership
    and their *knowledge* of Scripture and theology?

15. Answer 38 of the Westminster Shorter Catechism describes what
    will happen at the resurrection: "Believers being raised up in glory,
    shall be openly acknowledged and acquitted in the day of judgment,
    and made perfectly blessed in the full enjoying of God to all eternity."
    What does this catechism answer tell you about the "glory that is
    going to be revealed" (5:1)?

The Harder the Work, the Greater the Honor, pg. 216

Leaders aim to be faithful stewards of the portion God assigns. It is a
privilege to be God's agent, and the harder the work, the greater the
honor. We serve for the Master's sake, not for pay, recognition, power,
or rewards. Nonetheless, God promises a reward in 1 Peter 5:4: "And
when the Chief Shepherd appears, you will receive the crown of glory
that will never fade away." The Chief Shepherd . . . cares for the universal
church, and the elders shepherd their local congregations.

APPLYING THE TEXT

16. Did this passage help you to further understand the standards for leaders in the church? How might these instructions for church leaders apply to your own life, regardless of whether you are a pastor or an elder?

17. Why is it important for leaders to remember that the *Chief* Shepherd is coming? As you relate to church leaders, why is it important for you to remember that they are serving Jesus in their role?

18. Do you pray for the leaders in your church? Why is it important to pray for our leaders regularly? What direction can your prayers for the leaders in your church take from this passage? What are some specific prayers you can offer for them today?

PRAYER PROMPT

Now that you have considered the call Peter issues to elders in the local church, and the commands he gives to them, pray for the ordained leaders in your own church and in your broader community. Ask God to lead them to practice servant leadership, for his glory and for the good of his people —rather than for their own selfish ambitions or aspirations. Pray for him to help *you* to be faithful in whatever ways you are called to lead others—and to do so in consideration of the fact that Jesus Christ, the Chief Shepherd, will one day appear and that, when he does, all other shepherds must bow before him.

LESSON 13

HUMILITY AND BLESSING

1 Peter 5:5-14

THE BIG PICTURE

We have seen the instructions Peter gave in the opening verses of chapter 5, which called the elders of the churches to lead humbly, faithfully, and with pure, godly motives. These are now followed by Peter's instructions for *everyone* in these elders' churches to pursue Christlike humility.

Church members should display humility by remaining subject to their elders, Peter writes—by submitting to their godly leadership and direction. And they shouldn't stop there: an understanding of the opposition that God shows to the proud, and of the way he embraces the humble, should also lead Christians to clothe themselves with humility in all their interactions with other church members as well (5:5). Their commitment to humility, patterned after a Savior who humbled himself on the cross, comes with the faith-filled hope that God will one day exalt his people in glory, just as Jesus himself was gloriously raised from the dead and now reigns with God the Father (5:6).

As he closes his letter, Paul focuses on blessing his readers and giving them hope. First, he calls his audience to cast their anxieties on the God who cares for them (5:7). Peter then challenges them to resist the devil and to remember that the suffering they are enduring is a part of the same trials that their brothers and sisters in Christ are sharing in all around the world (5:8-9). He then speaks again about our hope for the eternity that will follow our earthly suffering, when God will vindicate and restore his people before inviting them to share in the glory and dominion of Christ their Savior (5:10–11). The letter ends with final words of greeting, blessing, love, and grace (5:12–14).

Read 1 Peter 5:5–14.

GETTING STARTED

1. Why do people often grumble and complain about their leaders, bosses, or supervisors? What sins tend to color the way we interact with authority? Which of these sinful tendencies do you see in your own heart?

2. Why is pride a source of significant damage to relationships and communities? How might selfishness and arrogance rip apart a marriage? A friendship? A local church?

We Must Remain Humble, pg. 229

In an essential way, the Christian *must* be humble, for faith begins with repentance. We confess, "I am a sinner, unable to reform myself, and without hope, outside God's sovereign mercy." While there is a definitive, one-time humbling when we repent, we must *remain* humble. Then God promises to exalt us "at the proper time" as he judges it (1 Peter 5:6 ESV).

OBSERVING THE TEXT

3. Go back and consult 1 Peter 5:1–4. What context do they add to your understanding of Peter's initial commands in this passage (5:5)?

4. In your own words, summarize the commands that Peter gives regarding the ways believers should speak and act in front of one another.

5. Throughout this passage, Peter balances his commands about what believers should do in the present with promises about what will take place in the future. What effects do God's promises about his people's future have on our behavior, words, and actions in the present?

UNDERSTANDING THE TEXT

6. What behavior does Peter command the younger people in the church to exhibit toward their elders (5:5)? Why do you think some readers would have needed to hear this command?

7. In 5:5–6, what motivation does Peter offer his readers for pursuing humility? Why do you think it is important for believers to await "the proper time" that Peter mentions in verse 6?

8. What does 5:7 remind us is true about our God? What does it say we should do with our cares and anxieties?

9. What does Peter say about what the devil intends and does (5:8)? What does this tell us about the nature of our battle against sin? Why do you think Peter refers to the community of believers in other parts of the world when he addresses the suffering that his own readers are facing (5:9)?

God Exalts the Humble, pg. 219

With tiny variations, Jesus says the same thing on three separate occasions: "Everyone who exalts himself will be humbled, and he who humbles himself will be exalted." . . . Both 1 Peter 5:5 and James 4:6 quote the Septuagint of Proverbs 3:34 almost verbatim, saying, "God opposes the proud but gives grace to the humble." Clearly, the call to humility pervades Scripture. In 1 Peter, it is the apostle's last word on leadership and the first in his series of closing exhortations for the church.

10. What hope does Peter hold out to believers who are suffering "for a little while" (5:10–11)? What encouragement do you think these first-century believers, who were facing ridicule, mockery, and scorn because of their faith in Jesus Christ, would have taken from these verses?

11. What do Peter's closing greetings within 5:12–14 tell us about the relationships he shared with God's people? What do they illustrate about what Peter has told us throughout this letter regarding believers' relationships with one another?

BIBLE CONNECTIONS

12. Read James 4:6–7 and note the connections between what James says in those verses and what Peter says in our passage for this lesson. Why do you think both apostles linked their calls for humility with warnings about the devil's intentions?

13. Read 2 Timothy 4:5–6, and note that Paul uses the same term that Peter uses in 1 Peter 5:8 ("sober-minded"). What kind of attitude and awareness does this phrase call Christians to have? Why do you think Paul goes on, as he is delivering instructions to Timothy, to remind him of the suffering he himself has experienced for the sake of the gospel?

THEOLOGY CONNECTIONS

14. Membership vows in many Reformed churches ask new members to commit to "submit [themselves] to the government and discipline of the church, and promise to study its purity and peace."[1] What does this membership vow do to apply the first command from 1 Peter 5:5? What happens when church members keep this vow? What happens when they do not?

---

1. The Book of Church Order of the Presbyterian Church in America (2019), 57.5.

The Abundant Grace of God, pgs. 237–38

How fitting that Peter, who betrayed the Lord and received the grace of forgiveness, closes his epistle by offering his churches the grace of God. His letter began, "Grace and peace be yours in abundance" (1 Peter 1:2). . . . The apostle's talk of grace is not formulaic. Peter denied Jesus three times, swearing on oath that he did not even know him. Yet when Peter repented, Jesus both forgave him and reinstated him as an apostle. Because of the depth of his sin, Peter loved the grace of God.

15. Bible scholars and theologians often make a distinction between the visible church and the invisible church. The visible church is made up of everyone who identifies as a Christian; sadly, not all who are in the visible church truly believe in and belong to Christ (see Matt. 7:21–23). The universal church is made up of those who are true believers in Jesus Christ, in all places and at all times throughout history. How does Peter emphasize Christians' belonging to both the visible and the invisible church throughout this passage?

APPLYING THE TEXT

16. Do you show humility to your spiritual leaders? If you do not, what might you do to show humility moving forward? What practical steps could you take to clothe your interactions with local believers with greater humility?

17. What promises in this passage offer you hope as you face suffering and challenges? What is God's plan for exalting his people? Do you think remembering this plan will help you to eradicate sinful pride? Why, or why not?

18. Peter's closing remarks—especially in 5:9—indicate the type of spiritual fellowship that we share with God's people around the world. Why is it important to remember that you are a part of God's global family of believers? List some ways you could connect more effectively with, and perhaps somehow encourage, your brothers and sisters who are facing hardship elsewhere in the world.

PRAYER PROMPT

As you finish your study of Peter's letter, thank God for the fundamental truths of the gospel that you have studied in this epistle. We are sinners who have been saved by the marvelous grace of God, through Jesus Christ, and who are called to love our fellow believers as we await Christ's return. Pray for the strength to resist the devil, stand firm in your faith, and endure trials and sufferings with Christlike humility as you follow in the path of your gracious Savior!

Jon Nielson is senior pastor of Spring Valley Presbyterian Church in Roselle, Illinois, and the author of *Bible Study: A Student's Guide*, among other books. He has served in pastoral positions at Holy Trinity Church, Chicago, and College Church, Wheaton, Illinois, and as director of training for the Charles Simeon Trust.

Daniel M. Doriani (PhD, Westminster Theological Seminary; STM, Yale Divinity School) is professor of theology and vice president at Covenant Theological Seminary. He is the founder and president of The Center for Faith and Work in St. Louis and a member of the Council of The Gospel Coalition.

"Among the large number of expositions of 1 Peter, this REC commentary stands out. It is exemplary in its careful handling of the text, theological robustness, and fresh writing. . . . This exposition of 1 Peter is loaded with the best kind of application: faithful to the text, reflective, never forced, often telling." —**D. A. Carson**

The Reformed Expository Commentary (REC) series is accessible to both pastors and lay readers. Each volume in the series provides exposition that gives careful attention to the biblical text, is doctrinally Reformed, focuses on Christ through the lens of redemptive history, and applies the Bible to our contemporary setting.

Praise for the Reformed Expository Commentary Series

"Well-researched and well-reasoned, practical and pastoral, shrewd, solid, and searching." —**J. I. Packer**

"A rare combination of biblical insight, theological substance, and pastoral application." —**Al Mohler**

"Here, rigorous expository methodology, nuanced biblical theology, and pastoral passion combine." —**R. Kent Hughes**